SACRED JOURNEY

A Pilgrimage to the
Stations of the Cross
in Jerusalem

SACRED JOURNEY

A Pilgrimage to the Stations of the Cross in Jerusalem

STEVEN BROOKE

INTRINSIC BOOKS
New York

Published in 2010 by
INTRINSIC BOOKS
c/o Specialty Book Marketing, Inc.
443 Park Avenue South
Suite 804
New York, NY 10016
www.intrinsicbooks.net

First Edition 2010

Library of Congress Cataloging-in-Publication Data available on request

ISBN 978-0-9718870-4-6

INTRINSIC BOOKS
The book packaging partnership between
Specialty Book Marketing, Inc. and Studio 31, Inc.

Cover photo: Station XI, Church of the Holy Sepulchre
Back cover photo: Station IX
Page 2: detail Station X, Church of the Holy Sepulchre
Page 5: detail, Station XIII, Church of the Holy Sepulchre
Page 6: Station X, Church of the Holy Sepulchre
Page 13: detail, Station III

Book design and production by STUDIO 31
www.studio31.com

Manufactured in China

Mater

Contents

Acknowledgments

I extend my deepest gratitude to those who provided funding for the original project, *Views of Jerusalem and the Holy Land:* the Graham Foundation, Chicago; Martin and Rosalie Kaltman, the Kaltman Family Foundation; Harriet and Marshall Harris, Harris Travel; and the Friends of the Bass Museum. I thank Laurie Bernard, Tim McCabe, and Lee Ann Ropes of Eastman Kodak for generously providing the photographic materials. For their support of these fund raising efforts, I thank Robert A.M. Stern, FAIA, Dr. John Varriano, Alan Aiches, Joseph Rosa, and Joyce Kaiser.

I am grateful to the officers and staff of the Albright Institute in Jerusalem (the American School for Oriental Research) for their assistance with the logistics of this campaign: Dr. Seymour Gitin, Director; Edna Sachar, Assistant to the Director; and Sara Sussman, Chief Librarian. I am especially grateful to Albright Fellow Glenda Friend who shared her knowledge and love of Jerusalem, and transformed me from tourist to resident.

I am indebted to the following for their suggestions and criticism. Walter Zanger, author and lecturer, fine-tuned the scope of the original book. His knowledge of biblical events and locations was invaluable. Dr. Dan Bahat, the former Chief Archaeologist of Jerusalem, put his encyclopaedic knowledge of Jerusalem at my disposal, and introduced me to many of Jerusalem's diffident gatekeepers. Any errors of attribution are entirely mine. Discussions with Albright Fellow Dr. Sandra Blakely were instrumental in developing the ideas of Sacred Site, Sacred Time, and Pilgrimage.

I wish to acknowledge those who assisted me at the onset of the origianl project: Moshe Goren and Nolly Ebert, Dr. Max Miller, Dr. Bonna Wescoat FAAR, Dr. Perri Lee Roberts, Wendy Watson, Rafi Gamzou (Israeli Cultural Affairs Consul in the United States), Donnis de Camp of Schoyers Books, and Ada and Clarence Cohen. I humbly acknowlege my long time inspirations: Richard Halliburton, Sir Richard Francis Burton, and my childhood mentor, F. Cleveland Test, MD.

I wish to thank the following for their willingness to allow photography when their places of worship were not open to the public. In Jerusalem, such permissions are not always easily obtained: Wadjie Y. Nuseibeh, Doorman of the Church of the Holy Sepulchre and Brother Edward, Garden of Gethsemene.

For my work in Rome, I rode a morotino, buzzing like a hornet through the Eternal City. In Jerusalem, the narrow stepped streets of the Old City preclude motor bikes; and lack of parking makes cars inconvenient. Therefore, appropriate to the city of pilgrimage, the photographer travels on foot, sharing both the pilgrim's sense of mission and ardor. Thus, I am most grateful for the hospitality of the merchants and residents of the Old City who, after seeing me on the streets each morning at 5 A.M., turned their suspicions to curiosity, and then amusement. Two in particular took wonderful care of me. Mr. Mazen Qaissi and his family offered their establishment as my own private khan and graciously accepted my family and me into their lives. Mr. Shabaan Amir provided me with necessary introductions in the Old City.

Patty Fisher and Kristen Damuth were invaluable in keeping my affairs in order during my stay in Jerusalem. Michael Leslie and Roland Joynes provided valuable technical assistance. My thanks go to my friends and family for their support.

I am deeply grateful for the assistance and support of my partners in this project, James Wasserman and Bill Corsa of Studio 31 and Specialty Books, and to Donald and Yvonne Weiser of Nicolas Hays who shared our vision.

STEVEN BROOKE
Miami

SACRED JOURNEY

Christian Pilgrimage in Jerusalem

"Let us go to the house of the Lord! Our feet have been standing within your gates, O, Jerusalem." —Psalms 122

All pilgrimage is rooted in belief in the sanctity of the sacred places where deities have appeared, or where Gods and Goddesses have intervened, or where deities have become human. Proximity to the center of the world is equivalent to proximity to the gods. Jerusalem, the holiest of cities "set in the center of nations" (Ezekiel 5:5), is holy to the Jews, Christians, and Muslims for what it is, for what it has witnessed, and for the vision of peace it represents. As one adage says, "We may speak to God anywhere, but He hears us best from Jerusalem."

Pilgrimage to Jerusalem is qualitatively different from pilgrimage anywhere else. Jerusalem is both the place of the miracle and the site for its celebration in architectural and ritual form. These rituals can be carried out anywhere. The worshipper is transformed through participation in actions and symbols that rely for their strength on their transferability, from one place and from one generation to another.

The actual holy spot, however, produces quite another level of ritual experience. Here the worshipper is transformed in two distinct ways. The lingerings of the original event impart mystical abilities to the worshipper to transcend time and place for experience with the original event, achieving firsthand what the local rituals attempt to recall. A second transformation occurs in the course of the journey itself, which is inevitably long, arduous, and exhausting.

The worshippers who travel this distance together experience the unique communal spirit of intensified unity of purpose, oneness of heart, and singleness of vision. The individual transcends the biological concern with survival of the self in order to experience the divine.

CHRISTIAN PILGRIMAGE

For Christians, pilgrimage has several distinct meanings. Historically, Jerusalem is holy to Christians because it was holy to Jesus. Jerusalem's messianic status was deepened by the miracle of the Resurrection. For St. Augustine, Jerusalem was a celestial vision of peace. And for Charlemagne, Jerusalem was a religious ideal, representing hope for a morally transformed and renewed society.

Christian Pilgrims were reported in Jerusalem as early as the third century C.E. Even without a Biblical command, pilgrimage became a major facet of Christian devotion. Pilgrimage was an attempt to recreate the lost world of the prophets, martyrs, and miracles. For many pilgrims, the only way to verify the truth of Christianity was to actually see and touch what was recounted in Biblical narrative. Only in Jerusalem could that be accomplished; only there could the Christian believer expect miracles.

Christian pilgrimage began in earnest with the uncovering of the Tomb of Christ in 326 (John 19:41). Constantine's monumental architecture built to commemorate the life of Christ expressed this religious allegiance. He considered devotion to Jerusalem as an expression of devotion to the humanity of Christ. This, in turn, generated the declaration of other holy sites. Christian pilgrimage centered on the Tomb of Jesus (page 74), even though the first place typically visited was the Mount of Olives, where Jesus was last seen by men as he passed to heaven. From there, Christians felt absolutely certain that they were standing where Jesus stood, and where, from the Garden of Gethsemene (page 26) or the area of the Dominus Flavit (page 22) they could see the Golden Gate of Jerusalem with His eyes.

Christian pilgrimage slowed during Muslim rule in the 600s but increased again in the 800s. Charlemagne encouraged pilgrimage to Jerusalem with building programs. Great waves of pilgrims came in the 900s and 1000s. The Crusades which followed were also envisioned as a pilgrimage, albeit an armed pilgrimage.

The dangers of Holy Land travel following the Mamluk era and throughout the Ottoman era nearly extinguished Christian pilgrimage. After sixteenth-century Reformation doctrine rejected its spiritual benefit, the practice ceased in Northern Europe. Pilgrimage did continue in Catholic countries of southern and central Europe and in the Orthodox nations. For Russian Orthodox worshippers converted to Christianity in the late tenth century, pilgrimage became an important feature of their worship.

Today, Orthodox Christians plan their pilgrimages around Holy Week and the Feast of the Assumption of the Virgin. Foremost is their presence at the Church of the Holy Sepulchre during the ceremony of the Holy Fire on the night before Greek Easter. Catholics come to Jerusalem for a personal type of inspiration.

Most visit holy sites, churches, and monuments, and find great meaning in the Stations of the Cross (pages 38ff) that mark Jesus' way through the streets of Jerusalem to Golgotha. Most Protestant pilgrims favor the open landscape around the Sea of Galilee, the Jordan River, the Judean Desert, the Mount of Olives overlooking the city, and the pastoral Garden Tomb in East Jerusalem. They try to imagine Christ as he would have appeared in the real landscape. Of course, many Catholics and Orthodox Christians visit these pastoral sites as well, and many Protestants follow the Way of the Cross, paying homage to the architecture and monuments that celebrate the life of Christ.

History of the Stations of the Cross

The Stations of the Cross are also known as Way of the Cross, Via Crucis, and Via Dolorosa. The history of the Stations of the Cross is somewhat confused as is the actual number. It is now settled on fourteen. The object of the Stations is to help people make a spiritual pilgrimage to the main scenes of Christ's sufferings and death. Chapels representing the important shrines in Jerusalem were constructed as early as the fifth century. However, there is no evidence that they were intended to follow exactly a specific Way of the Cross. Reports of fourteenth-century pilgrims mention a sacred route around the shrines but they do not identify a Way of the Cross as it is now understood. The earliest mention of Stations of the Cross occurs in the narrative of the English pilgrim, William Wey, who visited Jerusalem in 1458 and 1462. Wey mentions that pilgrims followed in the footsteps of Christ, but went from Calvary to the House of Pilate. By the sixteenth century, the accepted route was reversed to that which is followed today.

During the fifteenth century, pilgrims returning to their homes established a set of Stations by painting or carving scenes in monasteries and convents. The Stations were constructed in the Dominican friary at Cordova, the Poor Clare convent in Messina, and in Nuremburg. Stations were also located at Fribourg, Louvain, and Rhodes. Over the years, more imitative sites were constructed but there was no agreement on the number of Stations. Wey's fifteenth-century account mentions fourteen sites in Jerusalem; but only five correspond to current Stations, and seven are only remotely connected with the Way of the Cross accepted today. These were, the House of Dives, the city gate through which Christ passed; the probatic pool; the

Ecce Homo arch; the Blessed Virgin's school; and the houses of Herod and Simon the Pharisee.

During the sixteenth century, manuals of devotion produced for those visiting Jerusalem variously mention nineteen, twenty-five, and thirty-seven Stations. Jerusalem Sicut Christi Tempore Floruit, published in 1584, mentions twelve Stations and these correspond to the first twelve of the modern Stations.

Under Turkish rule, pilgrimage to the Holy places in Jerusalem was more difficult. This led to an increase in devotional ritual practice at imitative Stations throughout Europe. The current practice follows those European rituals of fifteenth- and sixteenth-century pilgrims.

Medieval accounts of pilgrimages make no mention of the Second Station or the Tenth Station. One Station mentioned in almost all early accounts, but not numbered in the present Stations, is the Ecce Homo Arch (page 44). One of the earliest imitative Stations indicates that Christ had nine falls; only three are currently included: the Third, Seventh, and Ninth. The other four stations correspond to four incidents: His meeting with His Mother; His meeting with Simon of Cyrene; His face wiped by Veronica; and His meeting with the women of Jerusalem. There is also confusion as to the timing of certain events. Some have placed Simon of Cyrene and the Women of Jerusalem at the same time while the Veronica incident is considered by some to have occurred just before arrival at Calvary.

In 1991, Pope John Paul II presented an alternative to the traditional stations as a way of reflecting more deeply on the Scriptural accounts of Christ's passion.

For some, legitimate doubts about historic accuracy are counterbalanced by the piety of the millions who add the force of their belief to sites already charged with the legend of sacred event. As countless guides suggest, the enduring power of such sites to inspire is best appreciated when seen through the eye of faith rather than through the microscope of history.

The sense of sacred site, embodied in the landscape of the Holy Land, can be felt in the grittiest streets of Jerusalem, sanctified by nearly 2000 years of veneration. The cumulative strength of that piety is palpable. And as we are reminded in Proverbs, "Wisdom cries aloud in the street." (Proverbs 20)

PRELUDE TO THE PASSION

Mount of Olives from Mount Zion

The Mount of Olives rises above the Kidron Valley to the east of Jerusalem. It is a mountain steeped in tradition. David retreated here to escape Absalom (2 Samuel 15:30). On the southern spur, Solomon built temples for his foreign wives (2 Kings 23:13). On his trips to Jerusalem, Jesus crossed the Mount of Olives to reach neighboring Bethany (Luke 10:38). Events prior to the Crucifixion are centered here (Mark 14:26–52). The Tenth Roman Legion camped on its slopes in 70 c.e. prior to its siege. In the wake of these events, the Mount of Olives has been a primary pilgrimage site since Byzantine times. Jews, Christians, and Muslims all have cemeteries here. This view is from the slopes of Mount Zion. The tower of the Russian Church of the Ascension marks the summit.

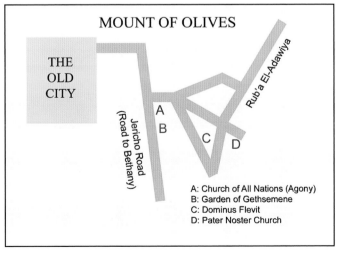

MOUNT OF OLIVES

THE
OLD
CITY

Jericho Road
(Road to Bethany)

Rub'a El-Adawiya

A
B
C
D

A: Church of All Nations (Agony)
B: Garden of Gethsemene
C: Dominus Flevit
D: Pater Noster Church

Jerusalem from the East, Summit of Mount of Olives

From the summit of the Mount of Olives, long considered to offer the best overview of Jerusalem, most the important geographical and architectural features of the city can be seen. From the left are the Hill of Evil Council (Abu Tor), the Hinnom Valley, Mount Zion

with the Church of the Dormition in the distance, the south and east walls of the Old City with the Aqsa Mosque and shining Dome of the Rock, and the East Wall with the Golden Gate at the far right. In the foreground are the gravestones on the slope of the Mount of Olives. At the left, just beyond the line of gravestones, is the southeast ridge of the City of David; to the right is the Kidron Valley.

Jerusalem from the East, the Road to Bethany

Bethany, "neigh unto Jerusalem, about fifteen furlongs off" (John 11:18), was the home of Lazarus and his sisters Martha and Mary, as well as that of Simon the Leper where Jesus was anointed prior to Passover (Mark 14:3). Jesus returned to Bethany after his entry into Jerusalem (Luke 24:50); and from Bethany he proceeded to Jerusalem

and his Crucifixion. The view across the Kidron Valley to Jerusalem has changed very little through the centuries. Climbing the steep ascent to Bethany "in the footsteps of Jesus" has always been an important aspect of Christian pilgrimage, in part because one can be fairly certain that Jesus walked this road and had a similar view of Jerusalem.

Dominus Flevit

Standing on the site of a fifth-century Byzantine monastery, this Franciscan church commemorates the site where on Palm Sunday Jesus "... *drew near and saw the city and wept over it*" (Luke 19:41),

and lamented its future destruction. Hence, dominus flevit, *"the Lord wept."* The modern church was built in 1955, designed in the shape of a tear by the Italian architect Antonio Barlozzi.

Church of All Nations (Church of the Agony)

This site, north of the Garden of Gethsemene, commemorates the spot where Jesus prayed before he was betrayed by Judas and then arrested (Matthew 26:36–56). Jesus knew he was in mortal danger (John 11:8) but that he could also retreat to the Mount of Olives and ultimately escape to the desert. Only through prayer could he decide whether to stand or flee. Pilgrims' accounts report a fourth-century

church on the slopes of the Mount of Olives which may lie beneath the present-day one. Called the Egeria (the Elegant), it is thought to have been built 379–384 C.E. In the eighth century, the Byzantine church was destroyed in an earthquake. In ca. 1170, the Crusaders built an oratory in the ruins which they replaced with another church that was finally abandoned in 1345. The present Franciscan church was designed by Antonio Barlozzi in 1924.

Garden of Gethsemene

"Then Jesus went with them to a place called Gethsemane; and he said to his disciples, 'Sit here while I go over there and pray.' He took with him Peter and the two sons of Zebedee, and began to be grieved and agitated. Then he said to them, 'I am deeply grieved, even to death; remain here, and stay awake with me.' And going a little farther, he threw himself on the

ground and prayed, 'My Father, if it is possible, let this cup pass from me; yet not what I want but what you want.' Then he came to the disciples and found them sleeping; and he said to Peter, 'So, could you not stay awake with me one hour? Stay awake and pray that you may not come into the time of trial; the spirit indeed is willing, but the flesh is weak.'" —Matthew 26:36–41

Pater Noster Church

Constantine commemorated caves associated with three events in the life of Jesus: his Birth in Bethlehem; his Resurrection at the Holy Sepulchre; and his Teaching and Ascension on the Mount of Olives. When the site of the Ascension was moved further up the Mount of Olives, the third cave was associated solely with the teaching of good and evil (Matthew 24:1–26:2). Queen Helena's fourth-century

Eleona Church was destroyed by the Persians in 614. The cave was venerated in the Crusader era as the place where the Lord's Prayer was taught and where Jesus spent his last nights in Jerusalem (Luke 21:37). In 1857 Princessa de la Tour d'Avergne bought the land and in 1868, built a cloister and founded a Carmelite convent. An attempt to rebuilt the Byzantine basilica in 1915 was partially successful. The cloister has the Lord's Prayer in 68 different languages.

Coenaculum, The Room of the Last Supper

According to tradition Jesus and his disciples at their Last Supper (the Passover Seder) in a "large upper room" (Mark 14:15; Matthew 26:17–29). The room we see today is on the second floor of the twelfth-century Crusader Church of Our Lady of Mount Zion. The bread and wine consecrated at the Last Supper became the

elements of the Christian Eucharist. This is also the traditional site of
the Miracle of the Pentecost when the spirit of God descended on the
Apostles who began to speak in "other tongues" (Acts 2:1–4). The
room was renovated in the fourteenth century by the Franciscans.
In the fifteenth century, the Moslems converted the room into a
mosque. The mid-1980s restoration preserved the Crusader arches,
vaulting, and columns.

The Prison of Christ

The chapel of the Prison of Christ is located at the east end of the north aisle of the Church of the Holy Sepulchre. First mentioned by Epiphanius, a monk of the eight century, the chapel was an early station celebrating the Passion and Death of Christ. A twelfth-century tradition holds that Christ and the two thieves were held on this spot prior to their crucifixion.

Vade Mecum

AN INVITATION
TO PILGRIMAGE

Traversing the Stations of the Cross is a journey made on foot—slowly, contemplatively. The entire journey can be made comfortably in two to three hours. Some experience the Stations of the Cross only once in their lifetime—perhaps the ultimate expression of their devotion. For many others, the pilgrimage is a daily nurturing ritual.

Tourists and pilgrims to Jerusalem typically travel in groups. They follow the Passion with friends and members of their congregation. The city feels the pressure of these earnest crowds often as early as 6:00 A.M. The times available for quiet, solitary contemplation of early twenty-first century Jerusalem grow increasingly rare.

However, for those willing to rise just before dawn, Jerusalem casts an ethereal spell. In the absence of cars, it is possible to hear an occasional footfall or a lone voice in early prayer. The forgiving light subdues the common and the abrasive, revealing, however briefly, the authentic and the ancient. It discloses portals to the centuries and inspires one to enter. Amid the echoes of three millennia, a singular moment of solitude in Jerusalem's ancient streets or on a hill overlooking the city, is indelibly hypnotic. I lived for those moments.

    With these images of Jerusalem I invite the reader to travel as I did—perhaps for the first time—through this mystical city, alone in thought.

    We start at the Lion's Gate (also called St. Stephen's Gate) and quietly enter the Via Dolorosa—the Road of Sorrow, the Way of the Cross, on our own private pilgrimage.

Via Dolorosa

The Stations of the Cross dramatize Jesus' last journey. Roman custom held that those condemned to death were obliged to walk through the city displaying the details of their crimes. The route followed today began to evolve in the fourteenth century under the guidance of the Franciscans; their original starting point was the Church of the Holy Sepulchre. Only eight stations were observed. Some are based upon popular tradition and are not mentioned in the Gospels. The present route through the Via Dolorosa was established in the eighteenth century, with Stations I, IV, V, and VIII agreed upon in the nineteenth century. At the right are the domes of the Church of the Condemnation and the Monastery of the Flagellation. The Ecce Homo Arch (page 44) is in the distance.

THE STABAT MATER

The medieval Latin hymn, "Stabat Mater," is a poem about the Virgin Mary and her profound sorrow at witnessing the death of her son, Jesus Christ. "Stabat Mater" is particularly associated with the Stations of the Cross. When the Stations are performed in public, as in church or an outdoor procession, it is customary to sing stanzas of this hymn while walking from one Station to the next.

Stabat Mater

VERSE 3

Oh, how sad and sore distress'd Was that Mother highly blest
Of the sole-begotten One!

VERSE 4

Christ above in torment hangs;
She beneath beholds the pangs
Of her dying glorious Son.

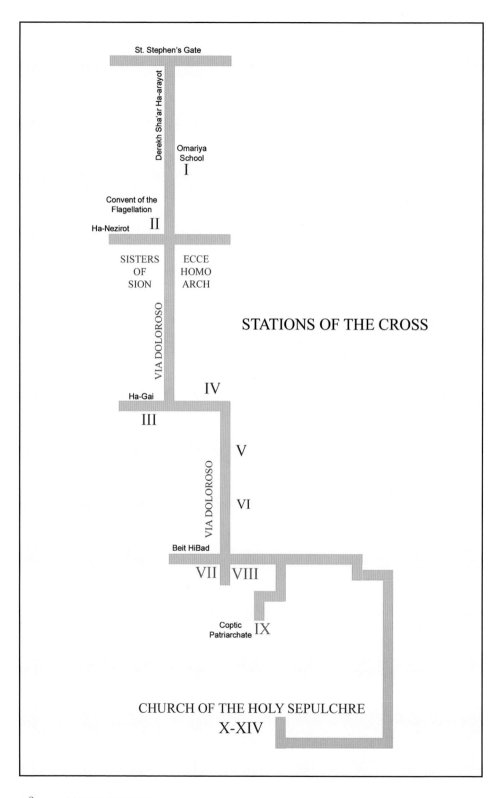

St. Stephen's Gate

Derekh Sha'ar Ha-arayot

Omariya
School
I

Convent of the
Flagellation
Ha-Nezirot   II

SISTERS   ECCE
OF   HOMO
SION   ARCH

VIA DOLOROSO

STATIONS OF THE CROSS

Ha-Gai   IV

III

V

VIA DOLOROSO

VI

Beit HiBad

VII   VIII

Coptic   IX
Patriarchate

CHURCH OF THE HOLY SEPULCHRE
X-XIV

THE
STATIONS
OF THE
CROSS

I

Station I: Jesus Is Condemned To Death

"When day came, the assembly of the elders of the people, both chief priests and scribes, gathered together, and they brought him to their council. They said, 'If you are the Messiah, tell us.' He replied, 'If I tell you, you will not believe; and if I question you, you will not answer. But from now on the Son of Man will be seated at the right hand of the power of God.' All of them asked, 'Are you, then, the Son of God?' He said to them, 'You say that I am.' Then they said, 'What further testimony do we need? We have heard it ourselves from his own lips!'" —Luke 22:66–71

Stabat Mater

VERSE 5

Is there one who would not weep,
Whelm'd in miseries so deep
Christ's dear Mother to behold?

These stairs lead to where Christians believe the Praetorium was located and where Christ was condemned. Scholars believe the Citadel is a more likely location. Now the Umariyya School for Boys, this was the site of the Antonia Fortress and other fortresses that guarded the northern side of the Temple Mount during the Second Temple period. It was the headquarters of the Roman garrison stationed in Jerusalem.

Temple Mount, Overview from Tower of Antonia

"They bound Jesus, led him away, and handed him over to Pilate."
—Mark 15:1

The view from the south-facing window of the Umariyya School overlooks the Temple Mount. With the Second Temple replacing the Dome of the Rock, this view is dramatically similar to what would have been seen by Roman soldiers stationed at the garrison in the Tower of Antonia—and by Jesus, if he had been detained here.

Ecce Homo Arch

The place beneath this arch is traditionally thought to be the spot outside the Praetorium where Pilate, referring to Jesus, said to the crowd, *"Behold the man;"* in Latin, *"Ecce homo"* (John 19:5). The arch is actually part of a triple triumphal arch once thought to have been built by Hadrian in ca. 135 C.E. as part of his forum in Jerusalem. Some scholars now believe it was built by Herod Agrippa (41–44 C.E.) in the Second Temple period. The north arch was incorporated into a chapel by the Convent of the Sisters of Sion (page 45); the southern arch was destroyed.

Sisters of Sion Chapel, North Arch

The north arch of the triumphal triple arch thought to have been built by Hadrian in 135 c.e. (but possibly by Herod Agrippa) was uncovered during a rain storm in 1851. The Sisters of Sion, founded in 1857 as an orphanage and convent, incorporated the north arch into the chapel that stands at the east end of their church. The Lithostrotos pavement excavated beneath the arch was also constructed during this period. Among the inscriptions carved into the pavement is the farcical game called Basilicus, or the King's Game. The rules, which involve heaping absurd honors on a "king" prior to his death, painfully recall the events of Jesus's humiliation at this point in his journey (Matthew 27:27–30).

II

Station II: Jesus Bears the Cross

*"Then Pilate took Jesus and had him flogged. And the soldiers wove a
crown of thorns and put it on his head, and they dressed him in a purple
robe. They kept coming up to him, saying, 'Hail, King of the Jews!' and
striking him on the face. Then he handed him over to them to be crucified.
So they took Jesus; and carrying the cross by himself, he went out to what
is called The Place of the Skull, which in Hebrew is called Golgotha."*
—John 19:1–3, 16–17.

Stabat Mater

Can the human heart refrain
From partaking in her pain, In that Mother's pain untold?

Station II is observed at the Church of the Condemnation in the Courtyard of the Franciscan Monastery of the Flagellation. Beneath the church are remains of a Byzantine church and sections of a second-century C.E. road thought by some to have been part of the Lithostrotos of the Praetorium.

III

Station III: Jesus Falls for the First Time

"I gave my back to those who struck me, and my cheeks to those who pulled out the beard; I did not hide my face from insult and spitting. The Lord God helps me; therefore I have not been disgraced; therefore I have set my face like flint, and I know that I shall not be put to shame; he who vindicates me is near." —Isaiah 50:6–8

Stabat Mater

VERSE 7

Bruis'd, derided, curs'd, defil'd,
She beheld her tender child
All with bloody scourges rent.

In the nineteenth century, Station III—not mentioned in the Gospels—was marked by a fallen column outside the Turkish bath house of the Hammam al-Sultan. In 1856, it was purchased by the Armenian Catholic Church. The chapel was renovated in 1947, funded by donations of Polish soldiers stationed in Jerusalem during World War II.

Station IV: Jesus Meets His Mother

*"Then Simeon blessed them and said to his mother Mary, 'This child is destined for the falling and the rising of many in Israel, and to be a sign that will be opposed so that the inner thoughts of many will be revealed—and a sword will pierce your own soul too.' His mother treasured all these things in her heart." —*Luke 2:34–35; 51

Stabat Mater

VERSE 8

For the sins of His own nation,
Saw Him hang in desolation,
Till His spirit forth He sent.

At the site of the Armenian-Catholic Church of Our Lady of the Spasm, Mary is believed to have spoken to Jesus on the way to the crucifixion. The church was built in 1881 and stands on Byzantine-era ruins, possibly those of St. Sophia (Holy Wisdom). A large mosaic was also discovered in the crypt at the level of the ancient street. The center of the mosaic depicted a pair of sandals indicating where Mary was believed to have been standing.

Station V: Jesus is Helped by Simon of Cyrene

"They compelled a passer-by, who was coming in from the country, to carry his cross; it was Simon of Cyrene, the father of Alexander and Rufus." —Mark 15:21; also Matthew 27:32 and Luke 23:26.

Stabat Mater

VERSE 9

O thou Mother! fount of love!
Touch my spirit from above;
Make my heart with thine accord.

This event is celebrated at the oratory built by the Franciscans in 1895 on the site of their first convent in Jerusalem (ca. 1229–1244). At this point, the Via Dolorosa begins its steep ascent to Calvary.

VI

Station VI: Veronica Wipes the Face of Jesus

*"Just as there were many who were astonished at him—so marred was his appearance, beyond human semblance, and his form beyond that of mortals—so he shall startle many nations; kings shall shut their mouths because of him." —*Isaiah 52:14–15

*"'Come,' my heart says, 'seek his face!' Your face, Lord, do I seek. Do not hide your face from me." —*Psalm 27:8–9

Stabat Mater

VERSE 10

Make me feel as thou hast felt;
Make my soul to glow and melt
With the love of Christ our Lord.

A Greek-Catholic church marks the site where Veronica, a Jerusalem woman, is said to have wiped the face of Jesus. The event is not mentioned in the Gospels. His image was said to have been impressed upon the veil, and subsequent healing powers were recounted. Since 707, it has been kept at St. Peter's in Rome. The Church of St. Veronica, partly owned by the Order of the Little Sisters of Jesus, was built in 1882 over the ruins of the monastery of Saints Cosmas and Damian (ca. 548–563).

VII

Station VII: Jesus Falls The Second Time

"Surely he has borne our infirmities and carried our diseases; yet we accounted him stricken, struck down by God, and afflicted. But he was wounded for our transgressions, crushed for our iniquities; upon him was the punishment that made us whole, and by his bruises we are healed."
—Isaiah 53:4–5

Stabat Mater

VERSE 11

Holy Mother! pierce me through;
In my heart each wound renew
Of my Saviour crucified.

The place where Jesus is said to have again fallen under the weight of the Cross is venerated where the Via Dolorosa meets the Suq Khan ez-Zeit. Though not mentioned in the Gospels, tradition holds that here, at the Porta Judicarta (Gate of Judgement), the sentence of death was posted. There are two stacked Franciscan chapels on the site; the lower chapel contains a red monolith where a street crossed the Hadrianic-era Cardo Maximus. It is probably through a gate in this area that Jesus left the city for Golgotha. Station VII was included in the fourteenth century to show pilgrims that the place of crucifixion and burial was outside the city.

VIII

Station VIII: Jesus Consoles the Women of Jerusalem

"A great number of the people followed him, and among them were women who were beating their breasts and wailing for him. But Jesus turned to them and said, 'Daughters of Jerusalem, do not weep for me, but weep for yourselves and for your children. For the days are surely coming when they will say, "Blessed are the barren, and the wombs that never bore, and the breasts that never nursed." Then they will begin to say to the mountains, "Fall on us"; and to the hills, "Cover us." For if they do this when the wood is green, what will happen when it is dry?'" —Luke 23:27–31.

Stabat Mater

VERSE 12

Let me share with thee His pain,
Who for all my sins was slain,
Who for me in torments died.

Station VIII, also believed to have been outside the city walls, is marked by a Latin cross on the wall of the Greek monastery. Around the cross are the Greek letters ICXC NI KA, representing the words "Jesus the Christian is victorious."

IX

Station IX: Jesus Falls for the Third Time

"Come to me, all you that are weary and are carrying heavy burdens, and I will give you rest. Take my yoke upon you, and learn from me; for I am gentle and humble in heart, and you will find rest for your souls. For my yoke is easy, and my burden is light." —Matthew 11:28–30

"Therefore I will hope in him. For the Lord will not reject for ever. Although he causes grief, he will have compassion according to the abundance of his steadfast love; for he does not willingly afflict or grieve anyone." —Lamentations 3:24:31–33

Stabat Mater

VERSE 13

Let me mingle tears with thee,
Mourning Him who mourn'd for me,
All the days that I may live.

Often difficult for travelers to find the first time, Station IX is reached by ascending a flight of steps off Khan ez-Zeit street and following a winding lane that leads to the Coptic Patriarchate, adjacent to the Coptic Chapel of St. Helena. A stone column marks the site where Jesus is said to have fallen a third time in sight of the place of crucifixion. It is not mentioned in the Gospels. The entrance on the left leads to a terrace occupied by the community of Ethiopian monks. Also on the terrace is the cupola of the Chapel of St. Helena in the Church of the Holy Sepulchre. The remaining stations are celebrated at the Church of the Holy Sepulchre (see inset map on page 63).

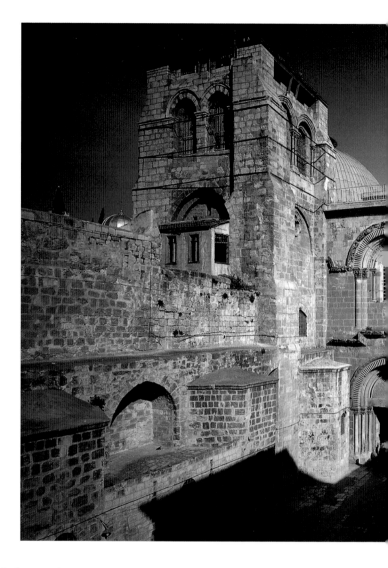

Church of the Holy Sepulchre

In ca. 326, St. Helena, the mother of Constantine the Great, built the first church on the site of the crucifixion and burial of Jesus as described in the Gospels (Matthew 27:32–3; 28:11; John 19:11, 41–42). It consisted of a basilica and rotunda. Destroyed by Persian invaders in 614, it was immediately rebuilt. In 1009, it was destroyed by the Egyptian caliph el-Hakim.

In 1149, the Crusaders rebuilt the church, to about two-thirds the size of the original Byzantine-era edifice, placing all the shrines under this structure. The church stands ca. 230 meters outside the first north wall of first-century Jerusalem.

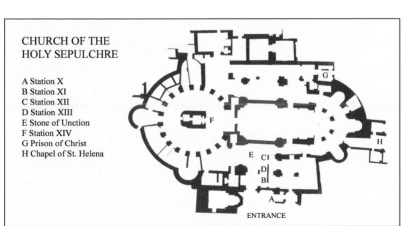

CHURCH OF THE HOLY SEPULCHRE

A Station X
B Station XI
C Station XII
D Station XIII
E Stone of Unction
F Station XIV
G Prison of Christ
H Chapel of St. Helena

ENTRANCE

X

Station X: Jesus is Stripped of His Garments

"And they cast lots to divide his clothing. And the people stood by, watching; but the leaders scoffed at him, saying, 'He saved others; let him save himself if he is the Messiah of God, his chosen one!' The soldiers also mocked him." —Luke 23:34–36

Stabat Mater

VERSE 14

By the cross with thee to stay, There with thee to weep and pray. Is all I ask of thee to give.

Stairs to the right of the main entrance lead to the Crusader Chapel of the Franks, originally built to provide a proper entrance to Calvary. It was closed following the fall of Jerusalem in 1187. Today, this two-story chapel contains the Greek Chapel of St. Mary of Egypt below, and the Latin Chapel of the Agony of the Virgin above. The interior of the former, can be seen from inside the Church of the Holy Sepulchre from the Latin chapel marking Station XI.

XI

Station XI Calvary: Jesus is Nailed to the Cross

"When they came to the place that is called The Skull, they crucified Jesus there with the criminals, one on his right and one on his left. Then Jesus said, 'Father, forgive them; for they do not know what they are doing.'"
—Luke 23:33–34

"Standing near the cross of Jesus were his mother, and his mother's sister, Mary the wife of Clopas, and Mary Magdalene. When Jesus saw his mother and the disciple whom he loved standing beside her, he said to his mother, 'Woman, here is your son.' Then he said to the disciple, 'Here is your mother.' And from that hour the disciple took her into his own home."
—John 19:25–27.

Stabat Mater

VERSE 15
Virgin of all virgins best,
Listen to my fond request
Let me share thy grief divine.

In the right hand nave of Calvary is the Latin Chapel commemorating the place where Jesus was nailed to the Cross in sight of His Mother. It was completely remodeled in 1937.

Station XII Calvary: Jesus Dies on the Cross

"It was now about noon, and darkness came over the whole land until three in the afternoon, while the sun's light failed; and the curtain of the temple was torn in two. Then Jesus, crying with a loud voice, said, 'Father, into your hands I commend my spirit.' Having said this, he breathed his last."
—Luke 23:44–46

"And about three o'clock Jesus cried with a loud voice, 'Eli, Eli, lema sabachthani?' that is, 'My God, my God, why have you forsaken me?' Then Jesus cried again with a loud voice and breathed his last." —Matthew 27:46, 50.

Stabat Mater

VERSE 16

Let me, to my latest breath,
In my body bear the death
Of that dying Son of thine.

The Greek Altar in the left hand nave of Calvary stands over the Rock of Calvary where it is believed the Cross stood. The rock, itself, can be touched beneath the altar. Since the fourth century, worshippers have held this to be the site of the Crucifixion.

Station XIII Calvary:
Jesus Is Taken Down From The Cross

"When it was evening, there came a rich man from Arimathea, named Joseph, who was also a disciple of Jesus. He went to Pilate and asked for the body of Jesus; then Pilate ordered it to be given to him."
—Matthew 27:57–58

Stabat Mater

VERSE 17

Wounded with His every wound,
Steep my soul till it hath swoon'd
In His very blood away.

The Franciscans celebrate this event with a small altar between Stations XI and XII. Called the Stabat Mater, it is adorned with a sixteenth-century icon of Mary sent from Lisbon in 1778. The icon recalls Mary's grief and symbolizes the eternal grief of all mothers at the deaths of their sons.

The Stone of Unction

In the eleventh century, there was a chapel to Our Lady over this site. The Stone of Unction, which first appeared in the twelfth century, represents the anointing of the body of Jesus prior to burial (John 19:38–40 and Matthew 27:57–61). Its position at the entrance to the Church was secured in the fourteenth century. The present stone dates from 1810.

Stabat Mater

VERSE 16

Let me, to my latest breath,
In my body bear the death
Of that dying Son of thine.

Station XIV: Jesus is Laid in the Tomb

"So Joseph took the body and wrapped it in a clean linen cloth and laid it in his own new tomb, which he had hewn in the rock. He then rolled a great stone to the door of the tomb and went away." —Matthew 27:59–60.

Stabat Mater

VERSE 18

Be to me, O Virgin, nigh,
Lest in flames I burn and die,
In His awful Judgment day.

In the dimly lit fourth-century Rotunda of Constantine, is the site of Jesus's burial and resurrection, the central shrine of Christendom. The monument over the tomb dates from the nineteenth century, one of a series of replacements for the original destroyed by el-Hakim in 1009. The present-day columns and piers are in the same positions as the twelve columns and eight piers of the original fourth-century structure. The dome replaced the one destroyed in the great fire of 1808. Heavy buttressing was necessary after the earthquake of 1927. The original tomb quite probably was located in this area which was a first-century Jewish cemetery.

The Chapel of St. Helena

Twenty-nine steps lead down over five meters from the main level of the Church of the Holy Sepulchre to the Chapel of St. Helena (the Armenian Chapel of Krigor, or Gregory). Thirteen more steps lead to an ancient cistern, now called the Chapel of the Finding of the Holy Cross, where St. Helena is reputed to have found the True Cross and those of the thieves crucified with Jesus. Some question this tradition because the story was only first mentioned in ca. 351, years after the church was built. The crypt did not exist in the fourth century, but was built by the Crusaders in the twelfth century. The north and south walls are part of the foundation of the Constantinian church. The Chapel was renovated in 1950.

Bibliography and Suggested Reading

Aharoni, Y. et. al. *The Macmillan Bible Atlas*. New York: Macmillan, 1993

Armstrong, Karen. *Jerusalem: One City, Three Faiths*. New York: Alfred A. Knopf, 1966

Atil, E., et. al., eds., *Voyages and Visions*. Seattle: University of Washington Press, 1995

Bahat, Dan. *The Illustrated Atlas of Jerusalem*. New York: Simon and Schuster, 1990

Barclay, J. T. *City of the Great King*. London: Challen and Sons, 1858

Brooke, Steven. *Views of Jerusalem and the Holy Land*; New York: Rizzoli, 1997

Davis, John. *The Landscape of Belief*. Princeton: Princeton University Press. 1989

Eliade, Mircea. *The Sacred and the Profane*. New York: Harcourt Brace Javanovich, 1959

Freeman-Grenville, G. S. P. *The Holy Land*. New York: Continuum Publishing Co., 1996

Kenyon, Kathleen. *Digging Up Jerusalem*. London: Ernest Benn,1974

Nir, Yeshayahu, *The Bible and the Image*. Philadelphia: University of Pennsylvania Press, 1985

Peters, F. E. *Jerusalem*. Princeton: Princeton University Press, 1985

Shanks, Hershel. *Jerusalem, An Archaeological Biography*. New York: Random House, 1995

Roberts, David. *The Holy Land*. Jerusalem: Steimatzky Ltd., 1994

Said, Edward W. *Orientalism*. New York: Vintage Books, 1979

Stebbing, Henry. *The Christian in Palestine*. London: Virtue & Co., 1858

Stewart, A., transl. Theoderich, *Guide to the Holy Land (1223)*. New York: Italica Press, 1986

Thompson, W. M. *The Land of the Book*. New York: Harper & Bros., 1882

Turner, V. and Turner, Edith L. B., *Image and Pilgrimage in Christian Culture*. New York: Columbia University Press, 1978

Turner, V. *The Ritual Process*. New York: Gruyter, 1969

About the Author

Steven Brooke, a graduate of the University of Michigan, is a Fellow of the American Academy in Rome, a Fellow of the Albright Institute in Jerusalem, a winner of the AIA National Honor Award for Photography and three Graham Foundation Grants. His books on architecture include landmark books on the Miami Beach Art Deco District, the influential town of Seaside, Florida, as well as the definitive book on the houses of Philip Johnson. His highly acclaimed books on Rome and Jerusalem, photographed in the tradition of the eighteenth- and nineteenth- century view-painters of Europe, were the first of their kind in decades.

Books by Steven Brooke

Views of Rome; Rizzoli International
Views of Jerusalem and the Holy Land; Rizzoli International
Historic Washington, Arkansas; Pelican Publishing Company
The Majesty of Natchez; Pelican Publishing Company
Seaside; Pelican Publishing Company, 1995
The Majesty of St. Augustine; Pelican Publishing Company
Seaside Style (with Lynn Nesmith); Rizzoli
Gardens of Florida (with Laura Cerwinske); Pelican Publishing Co.
Louisiana Gardens (with Mary Fonseca); Pelican Publishing Co.
The Houses of Philip Johnson (with David Mohney); Abbeville
The Houses of Marc Corbiau; Mardaga, Belgium
Miami (with Laura Cerwinske); Clarkson N. Potter
Deco Delights (with Barbara Capitman); E.P. Dutton
Savannah Style (with Susan Sully); Rizzoli
South Beach Style (with Laura Cerwinske); Abrams
Napa Valley Style (with Kathryn Masson); Rizzoli
Casa Florida (with Susan Sully); Rizzoli
Florida Modern (with Jan Hochstem); Rizzoli
Sonoma Valley Style (with Kathryn Masson); Rizzoli
Vizcaya (with Witold Rzbczynsky and Laurie Olin); U. Penn Press
Historic Houses of Virginia (with Kathryn Masson); Rizzoli
Miami: Mediterranean Splendor/Deco Dreams (with Beth Dunlop); Rizzoli
Aqua (with Beth Dunlop); Rizzoli
Great Houses of Florida (with Beth Dunlop, Joanna Lombard); Rizzoli
Great Houses of the South (with J. Laurie Ossman); Rizzoli
Views of Seaside (several authors); Rizzoli
Miami Beach Deco; Rizzoli